Anesthesiologist

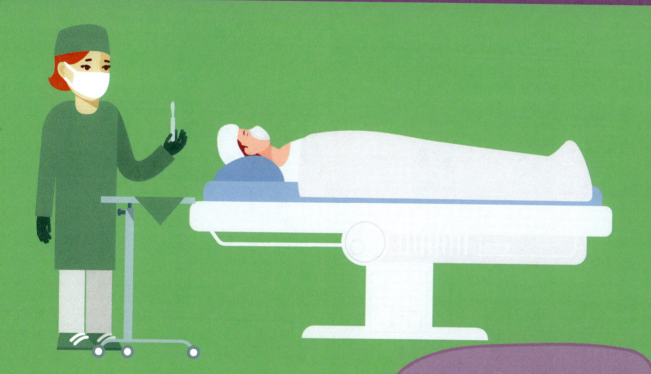

Anesthesiologists help patients sleep safely during surgery by giving special medicine

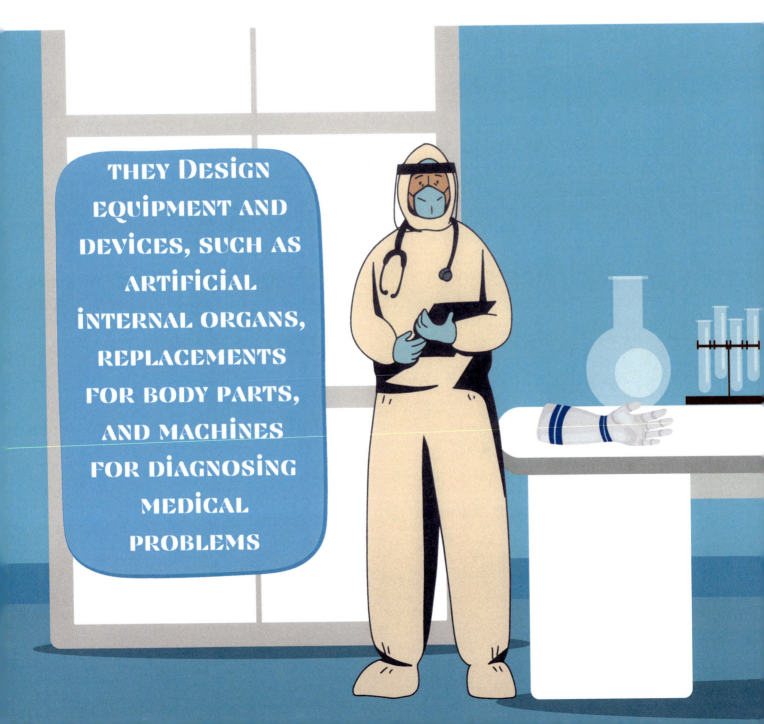

Cardiologist

A physician who's an expert in the care of your heart and blood vessels

Dermatologist

Skin doctors who help us with all things related to our skin, like pimples and rashes

Emergency MedicalTechnician

EMTs are real-life heroes who rush to help people when they are hurt or in trouble

Forensic Pathologist

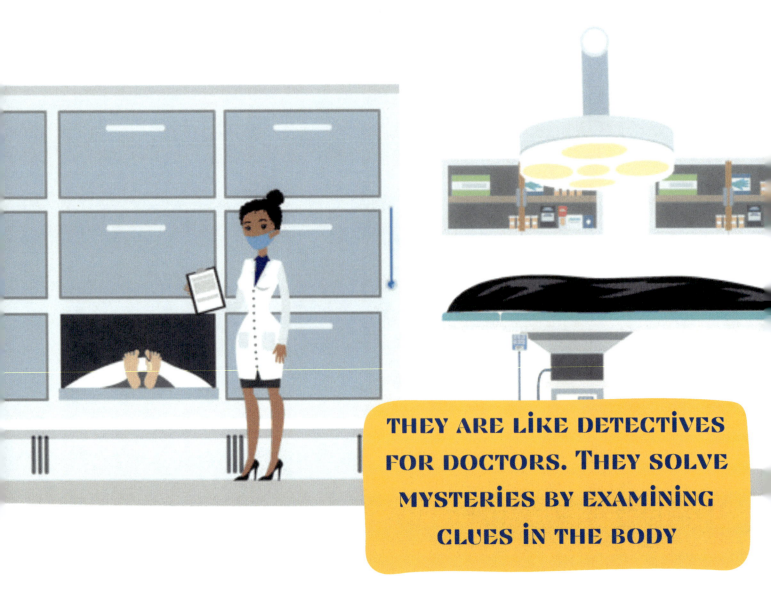

They are like detectives for doctors. They solve mysteries by examining clues in the body

Gastroenterologist

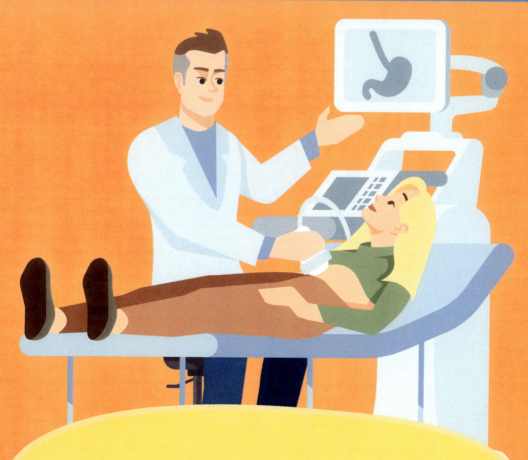

THEY HELP OUR TUMMIES FEEL BETTER WHEN WE HAVE TUMMY TROUBLES, LIKE TUMMY ACHES

Hematologist

BLOOD EXPERTS WHO MAKE SURE OUR BLOOD STAYS HEALTHY AND CAN HELP US WHEN WE'RE SICK

IMMUNOLOGIST

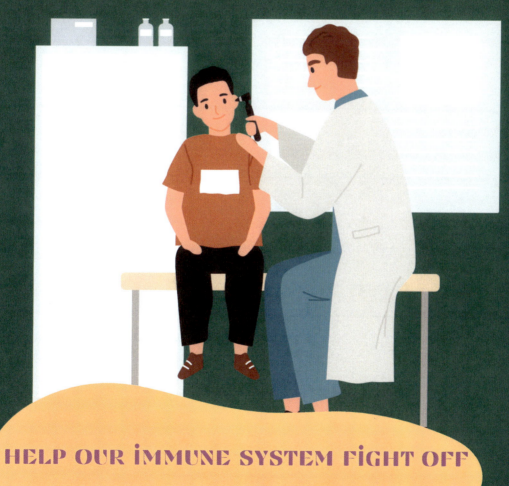

HELP OUR IMMUNE SYSTEM FIGHT OFF GERMS AND KEEP US WELL

JCAHO (Joint Commission on Accreditation of Healthcare Organizations) Accreditation Specialist

EXPERTS WHO MAKE SURE HOSPITALS ARE SUPER SAFE AND CLEAN FOR EVERYONE WHO VISITS

Kinesiologist

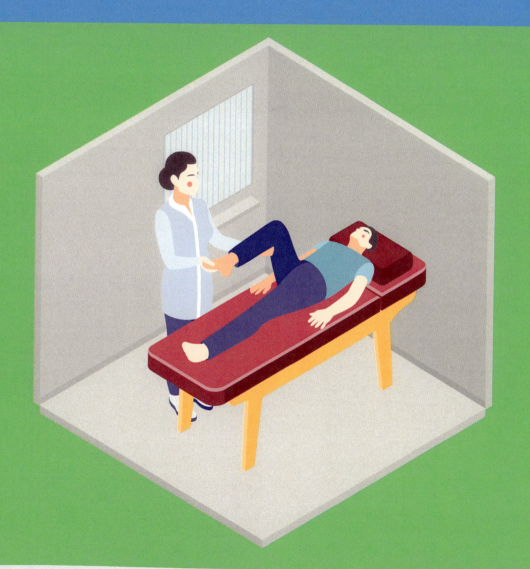

STUDY HOW OUR BODIES MOVE AND HELP US GET BETTER AT SPORTS AND EXERCISE

Licensed Practical Nurse

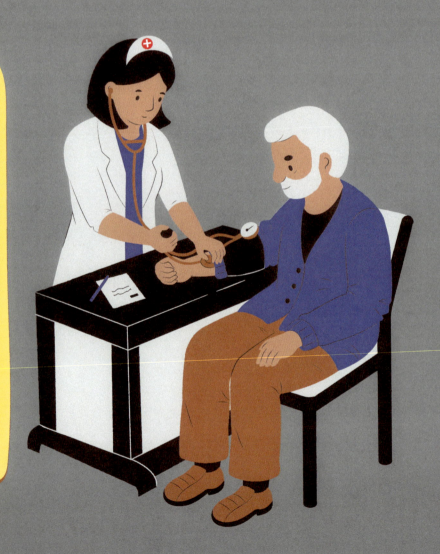

Licensed Practical Nurses (LPNs) take care of us when we're sick, making sure we feel better soon

Medical Assistant

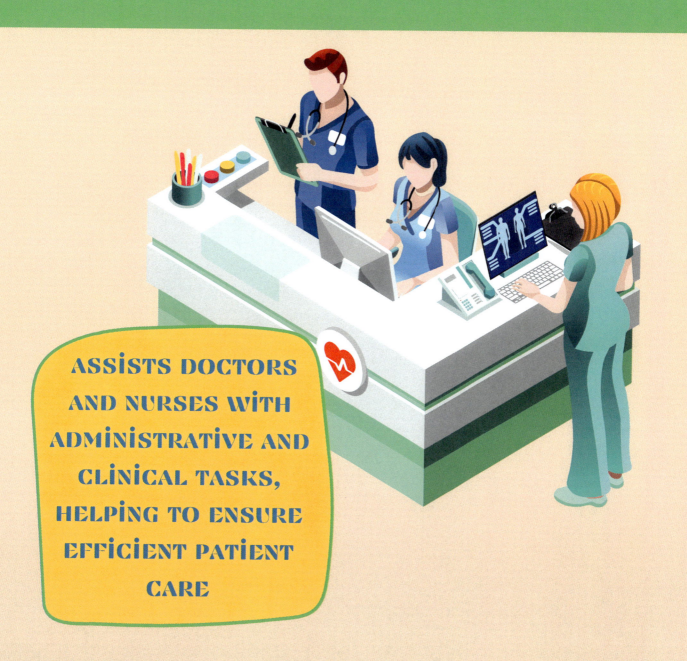

Assists doctors and nurses with administrative and clinical tasks, helping to ensure efficient patient care

Neurologist

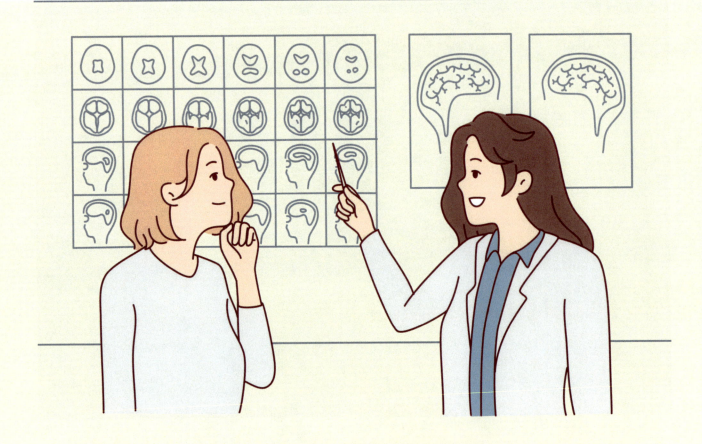

Specializes in diagnosing and treating disorders of the nervous system

Oncologist

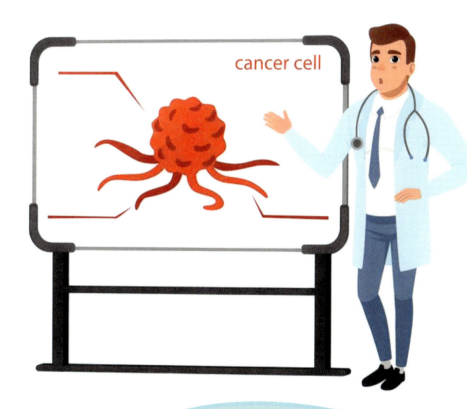

DOCTORS WHO HELP PEOPLE FIGHT A TOUGH ILLNESS CALLED CANCER

Pediatrician

KID DOCTORS WHO MAKE SURE WE GROW UP STRONG AND HEALTHY

Radiologist

X-ray wizards who take special pictures to see inside our bodies

Surgeon

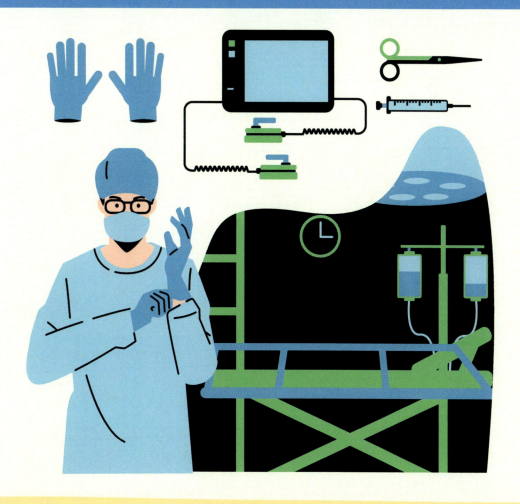

Doctors who can fix things inside our bodies with special tools and stitches

Toxicologist

HELP KEEP US SAFE BY STUDYING DANGEROUS STUFF LIKE POISONS AND CHEMICALS

Ultrasound Technician

Use special machines to take pictures of babies growing inside their moms' tummies

Veterinarian

ANIMAL DOCTORS WHO TAKE CARE OF OUR FURRY FRIENDS WHEN THEY'RE SICK OR HURT

Wildlife Rehabilitator

Help injured animals get better and return to their homes in the wild

X-ray Technician

X-ray technicians take pictures of our bones and insides using cool X-ray machines

Yoga Therapist

Yoga therapists use holistic practice from India, uniting body, mind, and spirit through postures, breath, and meditation for overall well being

Zoologist

ZOOLOGISTS STUDY ANIMALS FROM ALL AROUND THE WORLD, DISCOVERING COOL THINGS ABOUT OUR ANIMAL FRIENDS

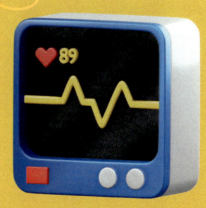

Made in the USA
Middletown, DE
20 March 2024

51485571R00015